TO MAKE A SPEECH

PACIFIC BOOKS
PUBLISHERS
PALO ALTO, CALIFORNIA

TO MAKE A SPEECH

BY
LAWRENCE H. MOUAT
San Jose State College

AND

CELIA DENUES
San Jose City College

ILLUSTRATED BY
GARY LAYTEN POST

Copyright © 1966 by Pacific Books, Publishers
All rights reserved
Library of Congress Catalog Card Number 66—28114
Printed and bound in the United States of America
Pacific Books, Publishers, Palo Alto, California 94302

This book derived from *How to Make a Speech and Like It!* by Lawrence H. Mouat and Celia Denues; copyright 1949 and 1957 by Pacific Books, Publishers.

PREFACE

Many changes, including one in the title, have been made in this edition, but the basic rationale of our original book, *How to Make a Speech and Like It!* (first edition 1949, second edition 1957) remains unchanged. The authors continue to believe that the classic canons of rhetoric form the basis of successful public address today, and that they can be taught successfully in the secondary schools. These canons are easily adaptable to modern society and can be expressed in the modern idiom. The brevity of the text and the illustrations are devices for motivation and for learning but not for eliminating essentials nor for watering down content. The goal is clarity, not simplicity.

Another reason for brevity is that the student needs all of the principles of speech-making as soon as possible, so that when he does communicate he can do so adequately. Naturally, the second time around should be better than the first, the third time better than the second, etc.

Suitable for a semester course devoted entirely to public speaking, this text is equally suitable for a unit on public speaking in a general speech course. Some schools have used it in condensed form for a speech unit in a regular English class.

The changes that were made were designed to strengthen internal consistency, to bring the illustrative material up to date, and to upgrade the instruction. The student today is better informed and more serious in intent than he was a comparatively short time ago, and he is more in need of training in the communicative process. The text has been adapted to meet this need.

April, 1966   L. H. M.
                                                               C. D.

CONTENTS

KNOW THE REASON WHY

Of all the means of communication
speech is the most important.

You may write
business letters,

    but

you use the
telephone more.

You may buy a newspaper
or a magazine,

    but

you spend your time
with your TV.

Much of your speech is automatic or informal and requires no special training

as when you
talk with friends and acquaintances

or when you
participate in bull and hen sessions.

There are many formal speech situations, however, that *do* require special training.

In school you may

—make oral reports in class
—enter the political arena
—conduct conferences
—speak out for a cause
—serve on a committee.

In the business world you may

—function as a club officer
—participate in local politics
—conduct neighborhood meetings.

In the professional world you may depend upon speech-making

—as a teacher
—as a preacher
—as a politician
—as a commentator
—as an entertainer.

Since there is every likelihood that you will find yourself in one of these situations, it is important that you know *how* to speak in public

—to do justice to your subject
—to yourself
—to those listening to you.

You can learn how to

—select, organize, develop, and present worth-while ideas
—speak audibly and distinctly
—speak with a clear and pleasant voice
—stand and move and speak with ease and confidence, and, above all
—communicate your message completely.

Here are the steps that will help you to do the job well when you need

TO MAKE A SPEECH

WHAT TO DO

The best way to get started is to get acquainted. Tell us who you are and then add something about yourself that will help us to remember you. You might relate a personal experience that will identify you. You might tell us about one of your enthusiasms. Whatever you decide to say to us, see if you can get us to make comments, to ask questions.

FIND YOUR SUBJECT
WHAT TO TALK ABOUT

Sometimes your subject is chosen for you, and sometimes you are asked to choose your own. In either case you will discover that the subject matter of a speech will lie in one of several broad general areas:

1. interesting *experiences* you have had, like
   —small-scale rocket-launching
   —mountain-climbing
   —school politics
   —job hunting
   —show business
   —rock-hounding
   —camp-counseling
   —pizza-throwing

2. interesting *places* you have been, like

—a famous building,
dam, or national park
—a museum with an
unusual collection
—an historical landmark
on the highway

3. interesting *characters* you have known, like

—an eccentric friend
or relative
—a stimulating writer,
or speaker, or artist
—an extraordinary athlete

4. worth-while *information* you have acquired, like
   —the meaning of meaning
   —the nature of the physical universe
   —marriage customs of primitive tribes

5. *controversial* subjects, like
   —foreign policy
   —civil rights
   —commercial advertising
   —science vs. religion
   —rules governing athletics
   —modern education
   —love and marriage
   —the welfare state

6. matters of *value*, like
   —the arts
   —literature
   —philosophy
   —a way of life

HERE ARE SOME PRACTICAL SUGGESTIONS

1. Buy a newspaper and turn to the editorial page. Find an article or a letter to the editor that makes you want either to *talk back to* or to *agree with* the writer. Do so!

2. Look at the titles of the articles listed on the covers of magazines in a newsstand. Do you see one that "rings a bell" out of your past experience, that makes you want to read it? If it meets with your expectations, buy it, digest it, add it to what you already know or believe, and talk about it.

3. Take a trip to the city or county jail, animal shelter, hospital. Ask to be shown around. Ask questions. That is your privilege as a citizen. What you discover may stir you to do some thinking, reading, and talking.

4. Attend a meeting of the city council, board of education, community forum, and listen to the debate. Which side do you agree with? Why? Think about it. Read up on it. Talk about it.

5. Take up a hobby—chess, coin-collecting, orchid-growing, writing, sightseeing, pottery-making, anything! Find out all you can about it. Then talk about it.

Be sure to figure out a "catchy" title for your subject. A good title will make us eager to hear your speech. Note the examples in this book.

HERE ARE SOME *DON'TS* AND *DO'S*

—Don't
  talk about something you
  know nothing about.

—Instead
  talk about something
  that interests *you*.
  If you are enthusiastic
  you will interest us too.

—Don't
  talk about something
  with which we are
  already familiar, or
  that is likely to
  bore us,

but
  talk about the curious and the unusual. Recent scientific
  discoveries and little-known facts of nature attract and hold
  attention.

19

—Don't
give us a predigested talk from a magazine.

—Instead
let your reading be an *addition* to rather than a *substitute* for your thinking. Talk about the subject from *your* point of view.

—Don't
try to cover too much territory in your speech.

—Rather
keep your subject within the time permitted. You would need all evening to talk on Our Foreign Policy or on Civil Rights, but you could handle Our Policy in Latin America or the Fourteenth Amendment in much less time.

WHAT TO DO

1. Make a list of five subjects you think y
   then make a list of five subjects you wou.
   someone else talk on. If you hand these to your insι.
   he will make one long list of suggested speech subjects
   and post it where you can refer to it.

2. To get practice in selecting a subject that you could talk
   on for five or ten minutes, take a broad general subject and
   make from it three specific subjects. Can you do this from
   each of these general subjects:

   —The United Nations
   —A College Education
   —Censorship
   —Alaska
   —Juvenile Delinquency
   —The Peace Corps?

3. Try to work out an eye-catching title for each subject you
   select.

DEFINE YOUR PURPOSE
WHY TALK ABOUT IT?

Your subject gives you an *area* for speech-making.
Your purpose gives you a *direction*.

Your subject is *what* you want to talk about.
Your purpose is *why* you want to talk about it.

What is it that you want to give *to* us or get *from* us?

Do you want to *entertain* us

    by

relating amusing or
exciting anecdotes,

    or by

describing intriguing or

unusual experiences?

Do you want to *inform* us

    by

imparting knowledge

    or by

giving us exact instructions?

Do you want to *persuade* us

to

make up our mind,

to

change our mind,

to

do or not to do something?

Do you want to *inspire* us

to

feel more deeply about something
we already believe in?

Your subject may be the same, but your speech will be completely different if your purpose is different.

24

FOR INSTANCE

You might choose The Hydrogen Bomb for a *subject*.

Your *purpose* could be
to entertain us by relating an atomic experience,

       or

to inform us about
    —how it is made
    —how it explodes
    —how it destroys

       or

to persuade us to do something about it

       or

to inspire us with the prospect of using atoms for peace.

You might choose Skin-diving for a *subject*.

Your *purpose* could be
to entertain us by
telling us some unusual
incidents that happened
while skin-diving

or

to inform us about

—the equipment used in skin-diving

—locating favorable skin-diving areas

or

to persuade us to take up skin-diving as a hobby.

26

You might choose An Outstanding Citizen of the Community as a *subject*.

Your *purpose* might be to entertain us by relating personal experiences from his life

or

to inform us of

—his influence on the community
—his achievements

or

to inspire us to

—work harder to overcome obstacles, as he did
—be true to democratic ideals, as he was.

You can't just *talk* on a subject. You have to have a purpose (or an object) in order to know what to *do* with the subject.

HERE ARE SOME EXAMPLES

1. Your *subject* might be Wishful Thinking.
   Your *purpose* might be to persuade us to keep our feet on the ground.

27

2. Your *subject* might be The Younger Generation.
   Your *purpose* might be to entertain us by comparing the warnings given to the youngsters of the "roaring twenties" with the warnings given to the youth of today.

3. Your *subject* might be Overcoming Obstacles.
   Your *purpose* might be to inspire us with the success story of a crippled war veteran.

4. Your *subject* might be Meager Salaries.
   Your *purpose* might be to inform us about how to live on a budget.

5. Your *subject* might be Photographs Worth Keeping.
   Your *purpose* might be to inform us of the rules to follow in order to have good picture composition.

6. Your *subject* might be My First Job.
   Your *purpose* might be to entertain us with unusual work experiences.

7. Your *subject* might be Driving Etiquette.
   Your *purpose* might be to persuade us to drive more carefully.

8. Your *subject* might be A Great Moment in Music.
   Your *purpose* might be to inspire us with the story of a musical creation.

WHAT TO DO

1. Take the five subjects you listed at the end of the last chapter and phrase a purpose for speaking on each one.

2. Take one subject and see if you can find three different purposes for speaking on it.

SELECT YOUR PLAN
HOW TO TALK ABOUT IT

After the *what* and the *why* comes the *how*. How are you going to handle your subject in order to accomplish your purpose? Make a plan—and follow it.

You need a highway map to follow in driving from Portland, Oregon, to Portland, Maine, from Boston to Baltimore, or through the Florida Everglades—unless you don't mind getting lost.

You need a blueprint for the contractor to follow in building your house—unless you don't mind having the bathroom fixtures in the clothes closet or a plate glass window above the fireplace.

And you need a speech plan to follow in making a speech—unless you don't mind losing us as well as yourself before you have gone very far.

Your plan gives you the *main points* of your speech.

HERE ARE SOME FAMILIAR PLANS

1. The Time Plan

> First main point—
>   what happened first
>
> Second main point—
>   what happened second
>
> Third main point—
>   what happened third
> etc.

Use this plan if you are going to

—tell a story
—trace events
—describe a process.

You might use this plan if you are talking on

—The Formation of the Grand Canyon
    (age by age)
—Putting Men in Orbit
    (step by step)
—A Day in Court
    (hour by hour)
—What to Do in an Emergency
    (minute by minute).

2. The Space Plan

First main point—at one location

Second main point—at another location

Third main point—at another location
etc.

Use this plan if you are going to describe

—a place
—a terrain
—a layout.

31

You might use this plan if you are talking on

—A Space Ship
—The Latest in Car Designs
—The United Nations Building.

3. The Theory-Practice Plan

First main point—the principle of the thing

Second main point—how it works

Use this plan when describing

—an invention
—an organization
—a structure
—a philosophy.

You might use this plan if you are talking on

—Color Television
—Your Student Council
—A Nuclear Reactor
—Existentialism.

4. The Problem-Solution Plan

    First main point—what is wrong

    Second main point—what to do about it

    Use this plan when

        —explaining difficulties and how they are overcome
        —describing a disease and its cure
        —arguing for (or against) a proposal or a policy.

    You might use this plan if you are talking on

        —How Man Was Able to Reach Outer Space
        —Is There a Cure for Cancer?
        —How Can We End Discrimination in Our Town?
        —Let Us Adopt the Metric System in the
           United States.

5. The Cause-Effect Plan

> First main point—the situation
>
> Second main point—its cause(s)
>
> > or
>
> First main point—the situation
>
> Second main point—its effect(s)

Use this plan (or both of them together) when pointing out who or what is responsible for the existing good (or bad) state of affairs and/or what will most likely result from it. You might use this plan if you are talking on

—Smog
—The Beat Generation
—Extremism
—Freedom Marches.

6. The Topical Plan

If your subject won't fit any other plan, it belongs here. This is the plan in which the main points fit into natural or logical divisions.

Use this plan when discussing

   —accomplishments or faults of men or institutions
   —rules and regulations
   —aspects, characteristics, or functions of organizations, products, machines.

You might use this plan if you were talking on

   —John Fitzgerald Kennedy—the Inspiration of Youth
   —The Los Angeles Dodgers
   —The International Game of Chess
   —The Experimental Theatre
   —The Morality of Civil Disobedience.

What do you think the main points for some of these might be?

HERE ARE SOME EXAMPLES

The Time Plan

Your *subject* might be The Terror of a Hurricane.
Your *purpose* might be to entertain us by describing a personal experience in one.

First main point—the approach of the storm
Second main point—the storm at its height
Third main point—the aftermath

or

Your *subject* might be The Show Dog.
Your *purpose* might be to inform us of the steps necessary to condition and show him.

First main point—training the dog
Second main point—grooming the dog for show
Third main point—handling the dog in the ring

The Space Plan

Your *subject* might be San Francisco: The City with a Personality.
Your *purpose* might be to inform us about certain spots famous the world over.

First main point—Fisherman's Wharf
Second main point—The remnants of the Barbary
Coast
Third main point—Chinatown
Fourth main point—the Presidio

or

Your *subject* might be Our Vanishing Forests.
Your *purpose* might be to persuade us that we are in danger of losing an irreplaceable heritage.

36

First main point—the forests of the Pacific Northwest
Second main point—the forests of New England
Third main point—the forests of the Everglades

The Theory-Practice Plan

Your *subject* might be Radar: Twentieth-Century Miracle.
Your *purpose* might be to inform us about what it is and how
it works.

First main point—the basic principle of radar
Second main point—its use in war and peace

or

Your *subject* might be The Honor System.
Your *purpose* might be to inspire us with an appreciation of
the honor system that exists at our school.

First main point—the code of ethics underlying the honor
system
Second main point—how it has worked in our school

The Problem-Solution Plan

Your *subject* might be Sudden Death.
Your *purpose* might be to persuade us to adopt a highway
safety program.

First main point—recent highway tragedies
Second main point—how the program will prevent needless
tragedies

or

Your *subject* might be The Treatment of Stuttering.
Your *purpose* might be to inform us of the most recent meth-
ods of treating stuttering children.

First main point—the nature of stuttering

Second main point—the therapy used in our local school
system

The Cause-Effect Plan

Your *subject* might be Soap Operas on TV.
Your *purpose* might be to entertain us by describing their influence on our lives.

First main point—some typical soap operas
Second main point—what certain people have done after
watching them

or

Your *subject* might be The Era of the Robot.
Your purpose might be to inform us of the great changes taking place in industry through automation.

First main point—the increase in the use of electronic devices
in industry
Second main point—the labor difficulties arising from exten-
sive automation

or

Your *subject* might be The Upsurge in Juvenile Delinquency.
Your *purpose* might be to inform us of a growing social problem and what has created it.

First main point—the alarming increase in juvenile delinquency shown throughout the country this past year
Second main point—this sudden increase traced to several
causes

The Topical Plan

Your *subject* might be Abraham Lincoln Today.
Your *purpose* might be to persuade us to practice Americanism as he would have done it.

First main point—Lincoln as a worker
Second main point—Lincoln as a good neighbor
Third main point—Lincoln as a realist

or

Your *subject* might be Jazz, the Player's Art.
Your *purpose* might be to inform us of the unique characteristics of jazz music.

First main point—basic emotions—the expression of jazz
Second main point—syncopation—the rhythm of jazz
Third main point—improvisation—the performance of jazz

Plans within Plans

You may need to divide your main points into sub-points. If
you do this, each series of sub-points would have a plan of its
own.

For instance

Your *subject* might be An Urban Renewal Program.
Your *purpose* might be to persuade us that the urban renewal
program in our community should be adopted.
Your first and second main points probably would follow the
problem-solution plan, but under the *problem* you could have
sub-points following a *space plan,* i.e., the various parts of the
city that have sub-standard housing; and under the *solution*
you could have sub-points following a *time plan,* i.e., the
sequence of steps needed to carry out the renewal program.

or

Your *subject* might be The Battle of the Bulge.
Your *purpose* might be to describe the progress of the battle.
Your main points could follow the *space plan*—the northern,
central, and southern fronts—but under each one you could

have sub-points following a *time plan,* a *problem-solution plan,* a *cause-effect plan,* or any other.

WHAT TO DO

You can practice

making out speech plans to accomplish each of the purposes you were asked to phrase at the end of the last chapter. State the subject, the purpose, the plan, and the main points.

It will help

you to be aware of the "how" of speech construction if you listen to speeches on the radio, TV, or before a live audience. Could you give a report to the class on a speech you have heard? State the purpose, and explain the plan used by the speaker to accomplish this purpose. How effective was the plan? Does it contain the main points adequately?

COLLECT YOUR MATERIAL
WHAT TO SAY

Now you know

> *what* you are going to talk about,
> *why* you are going to talk about it, and
> *how* you are going to talk about it,

but

what are you going to say?

You have already decided on the plan which gives you the main points of your speech. Now you are ready to develop them. What are you going to say under each point? What supporting material are you going to use?

You can't explain a point merely by telling us what we should know. You can't prove a point merely by telling us what it is we should believe. "He who asserts must prove." The builder must select good building material to make his building hold up. You must select good speech material to make your points "hold up."

Here are the various kinds of supporting material that can be used to develop each point.

Definition
    (what it is and what it is not)

Description
    (its appearances, functions, characteristics)

Authority
    (quotations about the point from persons, books, or existing beliefs)

Comparison and Contrast
    (what it is like and what it is not like)

Examples
    (specific cases)

Facts and Figures
    (sometimes called statistics)

Stories
    (real or hypothetical)

Statement and Restatement
    (points stated and repeated in different ways)

This material can be used to develop a point so that we will

—understand it

—believe it

—remember it.

Suppose, for instance, that

your *subject* is Efficient Personnel Management, with a *title*
Square Pegs in Square Holes, and

your *purpose* is to inform us about the development of a sound
placement program. You are using the

Problem-Solution plan.

Your first main point is
—an organization without effective placement.
Your second main point is
—what effective placement can do.

And suppose that

in your introduction you refer to your own experience in
setting up a placement program in your organization. You
tell us that you are going to describe the "before" and the
"after." You then develop your first main point (the problem) by giving us some examples of the waste and ineffi-
ciency that are due to poor placement. You give us some
startling production figures.

Now you come to your second main point (the solution)—
the new placement program. You might develop this point
as follows:

Definition

We licked the problem by adopting a scientific placement
program. Proper placement means fitting the job to the man
and the man to the job.

Comparison

It is like a jigsaw puzzle. Every piece is needed to complete
the whole, but it must fit into the right niche. If forced into

44

the wrong niche, it is not only useless but it may damage other pieces. The same can be said of the employees of an organization. When a man is in the right job, he is happy and efficient, and the firm makes money. When he is in the wrong job, not only will he be inefficient but he may hamstring others.

Statements

So here is what we did. We got a lot of pertinent data on each employee. We got this from tests and from interviews. Then we set to work and made some changes.

Examples

A second-rate supply inspector liked people much better than he liked materials. We placed him in the personnel office and now he is first-rate.

A routine clerk was going to be fired. We found that she had above-average intelligence, but was unable to use it and became bored. We gave her a more responsible job and she made good. On the other hand, a crackerjack filing clerk had been made a supervisor. Shortly after her promotion, we received some resignation notices. We discovered that as a supervisor she was out of her element. Her IQ was just too low. We had to fire her. Next time we won't make a promotion without checking the record.

Story

Then there was the case of the man . . . etc.

Again, suppose
your *subject* is Surfing, with a *title,* Romantic Rebels Without a Cause.

Your *purpose* is to inform us about the growth of this new sport, and

you are using the *Topical plan.*

Your first main point is
—who is the surfer?

Your second main point is
—what is his obsession?

In your introduction you might suggest that surf-riding may be the nation's fastest growing sport, a new enchantment for teen-agers and adults too, that it began in Hawaii and has become a minor mania in this country with the development of feather-light foam-fiberglas boards anyone can handle.

Then you might begin your first main point by asking the question: Who is the surfer?

Description

The stereotype of the young surfer is a tanned fellow with hair bleached yellow by the sun, dressed in loose knee-length trunks called baggies.

Definitions

He drives an ancient "woodie"—a wood-paneled station wagon with racks for boards atop. He and his pals speak a language all their own. A tumble is a "wipeout." The hollow of a wave is "the tube." A special big wave is a "grin." A chap who does acrobatics on a wave is a "hot-dogger."

Description and Figures

His treasure is his board. It is custom-made and costs from $100 to $200. Ends and sides are curved and tapered to his whim. Jutting from the underside of the stern is a sharp-edged fin, 6 inches deep, for stability.

The board is 9 or 10 feet long, 3 or 4 inches thick, about 2 feet wide, made of foam plastic-coated with fiberglas, decorated, maybe, and weighing about 30 pounds. It will zip 30 miles per hour on a good wave . . .

Statement

Some surfers are professionals.

Example

One of these who has extended his weekend hobby into a full-time activity is Mike Hynuson. Mike has ridden the waves of Africa, Australia, Tahiti, and has made 16 trips to the booming surf of Hawaii. Last year, he with others made a surfing tour from Rhode Island to Cape Kennedy, Florida. Mike is well known to surfing fans. He receives fan mail from the surfing set who follow his exploits in the sport magazines. . . .

Statement and Description

But the surfer is an ordinary guy, too. The sport has attracted a cross-section of typical American youth, and most surfers are likely to be average high school or college kids, set apart by their devotion to surfing.

Facts and Figures

Fifteen thousand turned out for a contest on a New York beach. The Great Lakes are more and more the scene of surfing safaris and, on lakes too small for waves, surfers ride on the wake of small boats. So many surfers turned out on South Beach in Miami Beach, Florida, that authorities there restricted surfing to 100 yards of ocean front. As in other sports, world championships are established.

In developing your second main point, you might ask: Why has surf-riding lured hundreds of thousands—teen-agers, sportsmen, young adults—like lemmings to the sea?

Quotations

Says one psychiatrist, "Surfing's lure for teen-agers follows a classic pattern of youngsters trying to be romantic rebels without a cause. Surfing fits the pattern beautifully, as the surfer—a tanned, graceful Galahad—is a heroic lure for young people searching for romance and freedom. Then, too, the sea is always an attractive symbol for wild, unbounded freedom."

But what do the surfers themselves say?

One girl says, "It's all feeling and sensation, a feeling of achievement."

A contest champion states, "You have a chance to prove yourself. If you get wiped out, there's always another wave, a repeated challenge. If you meet it head on and succeed, you feel real gratification."

An older surfer adds, "It's a release from the exploding tensions of the twentieth century, an escape from the hustling city of steel and concrete and a return to nature's reality, a special kind of madness, a feeling for the sea, a combination of love, knowledge, respect, fear."

Carter Davidson, president of Union College, spoke to the student body on the *subject* of Semantics.

His *title* was Common Confusions and his *purpose* was to inform the audience about ways to overcome confusion over the meaning of words.

48

He used the *problem-solution plan* and his main points were (1) Americans confuse many words and their meanings and (2) we can learn to avoid these confusions by developing our senses.

He began by telling a story, an incident taken from *Alice in Wonderland*.

Story

When our friend Alice took her famous trip into Wonderland, she was more than commonly confused by the similarities joined with differences in the Tweedledum and Tweedledee of the looking-glass country. Lewis Carroll was no fool, but a learned professor of mathematics, attempting to show his readers what a vast amount of discrimination is needed to distinguish sense from nonsense. In Alice's discussion with the Mock Turtle on the curriculum the Mock Turtle remarked that he had taken the "unusual course," consisting of "Reeling, Writhing, and Rhythmetics in all four branches: Ambition, Distraction, Uglification, and Derision." These sounded so much like the real thing to Alice that she was confused, and well she might be, for this was her first experience with the puzzling science of semantics, or the meaning of words.

Under his first main point, he had several sub-points:

Americans often confuse training and education.
Americans often confuse size and importance.
Americans tend to identify democracy and republicanism.
Americans tend to confuse money and wealth.
Americans tend to confuse preparation for life and participation in life.

Under the sub-point, the confusion between training and education, he said:

Definition

Training is clearly a process by which the pupil is taught to perform an act by imitating the manipulations of the teacher, doing it over and over until the act approaches perfection. Education, on the other hand, should acquaint the student with the ways of analyzing problems of all sorts and descriptions, so that his mind is keen to understand basic meanings and implications, and when he is faced one day by a problem he has never solved, or even seen before, he will be able to analyze the problem into its elements and proceed toward its solution. Education may use training extensively. The pianist, for example, will need to be trained in finger exercises and piano techniques, but he should also be educated in interpretation and expression. Don't fall into the confusion of believing you are educated in a field when you are merely well trained. . . .

Under the sub-point, the confusion between democracy and republicanism, he said:

Description

Many in our political world are confusing our minds about democracy and republicanism.

They are not the same. Our democracy refers to the spirit which pervades a society, which insists upon the rights of the individual; it refers to our freedoms—personal, intellectual, religious, economic, and political. Our republic, on the other hand refers to our form of government, which allocates responsibilities to its branches, the executive, the legislative, and the judicial; it sets up checks and balances between the federal government and the states, the townships, and the citizens; and it provides the machinery for effective social organization. Some persons in America have been saying that the founders of our nation were interested in establishing a republic, but had no faith in democracy. I insist that the same men who wrote the Constitution also wrote the first ten amendments, the Bill of Rights for democratic freedoms; the genius of the United States of America is that it has successfully combined a republican form of government with a democratic free society, almost unique in the annals of man.

Under the sub-point, the confusion between preparation for life and participation in life, he said:

Statement, Examples, and Restatement

Reflection and action must go hand in hand.

In the distant past we have seen the Emperor Marcus Aurelius meditating over philosophy in the midst of his military campaigns; we recall that Leonardo Da Vinci found time for painting *Mona Lisa* and writing sonnets while he was serving as city engineer. Johann Wolfgang von Goethe wrote the great philosophical drama, *Faust*, while serving as prime minister of the busy duchy of Weimar. In more recent times, T. E. Lawrence became a profound scholar, but was able also to manipulate and lead a revolt in the desert; Justice Oliver Wendell Holmes was a member of the United States Supreme Court while retaining a wide interest in every field of knowledge and culture; and Thomas Vernon Smith served with distinction in the Congress of the United States while a college professor of philosophy. These men give concrete proof to my thesis: we must combine participation with preparation, action with reflection.

In his second main point, Mr. Davidson asks: How then can we learn to avoid these common confusions, these mistakings of the show for the reality? I suggest that we must try to develop for ourselves two more senses, in addition to the five old ones.

Comparison

First of these senses is the aesthetic sense, or the sense of taste, which will reveal to us, after constant practice, the difference between the good and the bad in act and conduct. There are men who make a good living as "tea tasters," sensitizing the taste buds on their tongues until they can tell by the flavor the kind, the locale, and the grade of tea leaves. If the individual can improve his physical apperceptions to this point, he can do the same for his mental and moral state. . . .

Davidson then describes another sense, good humor. In his conclusion he referred back to his introduction, saying

Comparison

When we, like Alice in Wonderland, are confused and befuddled by similarities of phrase which conceal a vast difference of meaning, or by the clever misinterpretation of propaganda, let us call a halt and sift the true from the false, discriminate fairly, and apply our new senses of good taste and good humor.

A student gave a talk on the *subject* Fluoridation, with the *title* Save Our Children's Teeth! Her *purpose* was to persuade us that fluoridation of water is beneficial. She followed the *problem-solution* plan, and her main points were (1) tooth decay is widespread in the country today and (2) fluoridation of water is a major factor in preventing decay. After describing the prevalence of tooth decay in the country (the problem), she came to the solution phase. She said in part:

Statistics

Research was conducted on a larger scale. Some cities added fluoride to their water, and others stood by as control groups. Those adding fluoride over a period of years reported 60% fewer cavities in the 6-to-10-year-old group and 30% fewer cavities in the 17-year-old group. No mottling occurred.

Authority

These studies sound like a toothpaste commercial—where one group has 34% fewer cavities than the other, but the studies were conducted scientifically and were confirmed and reconfirmed by the American Dental Association, the American Medical Association, and the Academy of Dental Pediatrics, to name but a few. With all this evidence it should be possible to conclude that if within a few years all communities would adapt fluoridation of water the problem of tooth decay would be well on the way to solution. But although the benefits of fluoridation seemed obvious to many people, there are those who still raise objections. These must be met.

Facts

The first objection was the claim that fluoridation was a long-term danger. Accumulation of fluoride in the body over a number of years would cause an increased death rate, it is said, or at least it would aggravate diseases. But what these people do not seem to realize is that fluorides now exist and have existed naturally in varying quantities in the water supply of many communities throughout the nation, and considerable research reveals that there has been no more of an increase in the death rate or in various physical ailments in these communities with natural fluoridation than in those communities with no trace of fluoridation.

Comparison

The second objection appears to be an attack on "mass medication." But, again, if fluoridation of water is attacked on the grounds that it is compulsory medication, what about smallpox vaccinations, pasteurization of milk, or even the more recent chlorination of water? Fluoride, further, is not a medicine in the general sense but is a mineral that in its natural state has been discovered to be a staple element in our diet. Then, if the objection is raised that a mineral is not a food, why is there no objection to the mineral enrichment of flour and other foods?

Statement

The third objection, and probably the most prevalent, is the objection to compulsory fluoridation of water. It is asserted that those who want the fluoride should put it in for themselves and not force those who do not want it to consume it and to pay for it. This can be answered in several ways.

Facts and Comparison

First, if all property-owners are required to pay school taxes whether they have children or not, why should they not be required to pay for the prevention of tooth decay in children whether they have children or not? In both cases the children benefit. Secondly, fluoridation of water is by far the cheapest way to obtain the needed fluoride supplement; the cost is about ten to fifteen cents per person per year. Fluoride in the form of supplements would cost thirty-five times this amount! Lastly, water fluoridation is the best way to reach the most people. Fluoride to be effective must be taken at all times. How many children even when prodded by their mothers would remember to take a fluoride tablet 365 days a year for the first crucial fifteen years of their lives?

Restatement

I hope you are able to see that fluoridation is beneficial. As I have shown, fluoride does not increase the death rate nor does it cause or aggravate diseases, it does not constitute "mass medication," and fluoridation in other forms is not nearly as effective as water fluoridation. Fluoride is a simple decay preventative. These are the issues of fluoridation, and when the facts are reviewed rationally, without emotional interference, there can be no other conclusion than that there should be fluoridation of water in every community to bring about a safe, sane, inexpensive, and appreciable reduction in tooth decay in our children.

Suppose you are speaking to a lodge on the *subject* Social Action, which could also be your *title*.

Your *purpose* is to inspire the membership to meet the challenge of a world in need of help today. You choose the *topical plan* for you want to suggest different kinds of action as your main points. After appropriate introductory remarks you might develop your main points this way.

Statement

There is action and action—the right kind and the wrong kind. And there is inaction.

Story

Inaction is not conducive to brotherhood. Do you recall the account of the aftermath of the tragedy at the Indianapolis Auto Classic a few years ago? Two persons were killed and dozens injured when a portable grandstand collapsed. What did the people do who were standing nearby? They did nothing! They munched their hot dogs, they looked on the scene of horror, and then they looked away and finished their hot dogs. They didn't want to lose their preferential places from which they could view the race. Furthermore, they did not want to be involved.

Examples

There is inaction too, when someone else is called upon to collect bedding for the relief of the cold, homeless families in Chile, when someone else is supposed to vote for bonds for new schools for new kids in newly crowded districts. And there is inaction when someone else is supposed to prove that Americans are not intolerant by selling property to a member of a minority group.

Quotation

"Let George do it" is the precept of inaction.

Statement and Restatement

The *wrong action* is not conducive to brotherhood, either. Some people do nothing to relieve suffering, as was the case at Indianapolis, while others do the wrong thing.

Examples

People do the wrong thing when they slam on their brakes at the scene of an accident, not to render what aid or comfort they can, but to feast their eyes on the suffering of others, a nice morbid practice. People do the wrong thing when they give financial aid to worthy causes for income tax reduction or to impoverished countries either for a handsome return on investment or to counter the advance of communism but *not* just to be brotherly.

Quotation

"What's in it for me" is the precept of the wrong action.

Statement

Maybe I can best illustrate the *right action,* the life blood of true brotherhood, by the story of the "modern" Good Samaritan that is told at our school once in a while.

Story

One year when the annual football game between San Jose State and the University of the Pacific took place in Spartan Stadium this incident occurred. As the crowd of rooters on the San Jose side was hurrying out, one rooter was attacked by hoods, who were not college students. He was severely injured and left sprawled in the bushes by the side of the ramp. His fellow rooters glanced at him but continued on their way. They had dates to keep. Presently a University of the Pacific rooter who happened to be on the San Jose side by accident, hurrying along, also saw the injured man, went over and picked him up, got him out of the stadium, hailed a taxi, went to the hospital and did not leave until he had assured the office that he would assume financial responsibility if the victim could not. Then he went to *his* date. So now I leave you with this question: Who was the good neighbor, the fellow students who passed by or the rival student who gave aid?

Do you see now how various kinds of supporting material can be used to develop the points of your talk? Choose supporting material that will round out your main points until we no longer misunderstand them, distrust them, or forget them.

HERE ARE SOME SUGGESTIONS THAT WILL HELP YOU TO DO THIS.

Be sure your material is *clear*.

—Avoid unnecessary details.
—Use round figures.

For instance, instead of saying

Last year out of a total student body of 5,231 there were 489 reported cases of cheating in examinations

say

Last year with a student enrollment of just over 5,000 there were nearly 500 reported cases of cheating during examinations. This is a ratio of 10 to 1!

—Use *visual* materials to supplement your *oral* materials.

A *blackboard* will aid you

but

don't talk to the board

and

don't cover the board with your body.

A *chart* will help you

but

make it simple

and

be sure we can see it.

A *model* will help you

but

never pass models (or pictures) around the room while you are talking about something else, or we will find ourselves trying to focus on two things at the same time.

WARNING

Visual aids should *aid* you, not *replace* you!

Be sure your material is *interesting*.

We will be interested if what you say is *important* to us, if it affects

—our homes
—our health
—our earnings
—our prestige
—our comfort
—our beliefs
—our future.

We will be interested if what you say holds our *attention*. You can hold our attention by talking about

- —something funny
- —something unusual
- —some sort of conflict
- —something familiar
- —something nearby
- —something in motion.

Be sure your material is *appropriate*.

- —Will your audience accept your statistics?
    Are they recent, reliable, valid?
- —Will your audience accept your authorities?
    Are they recent, unbiased, competent?
- —Will your audience accept your arguments?
    Have you avoided being antagonistic?
    Have you answered the objections, the
    "yes buts," to your proposal?

Have you avoided being needlessly
offensive?

For example

If you were urging the city fathers to appropriate funds for
a drag strip, instead of saying,

We must have a place to "drag" our cars. If you won't pro-
vide us with a place, don't complain if we use the back
streets . . .

you might say,

A drag strip will give us a place to race our cars without en-
dangering other people. An adequate strip will encourage
us to take pride in our cars and in keeping them always in
the best running condition.

or

If you are urging students to buy bids for the coming prom,
instead of saying,

If you students had any school spirit, you would buy bids
to this dance. If the attendance at our dances gets any
poorer, we are going to discontinue having them . . .

you might say,

Buy a bid and have fun at our all-school dance. If enough
bids are sold we will replace the records with a live dance
band.

or

If you are speaking for higher taxes before an economy-
minded city council, instead of saying,

You men are afraid that you won't be re-elected if you put
through this new tax rate . . .

you might say,

> We are proud of our city. Our schools, our library, our parks all pay tribute to the men who had the courage to create them. There remains but one more job—to provide a recreation center for our children. Our tax rate will go up, yes, but our delinquency rate will go down and stay down. Our taxpayers will not shirk this greatest of all responsibilities. You must not shirk yours.

—Will your audience accept you, yourself, as being the proper person to present this material?

> Can you convince them of your competency?
> Can you convince them of your honesty?
> Emerson once said of a speaker, "What you are thunders so loudly, I cannot hear what you say."

WHAT TO DO

1. Look through magazines and newspapers until you find some material that interests you. Bring to class several articles; label them according to the kind of supporting material they contain and keep them in a folder where you can find them later when preparing a speech.

2. Listen to the conversations of your friends and to commentators on the radio or TV. When you hear of an unusual experience, write it down, using a conversational style that suits you. Keep it to use later in a speech.

3. Look in your library for a book of quotations. You will probably find Stevenson's *Home Book of Quotations* or else Bartlett's *Familiar Quotations*. Turn to a subject that appeals to you and find three quotations you consider outstanding.

   Also, look and listen for quotations from prominent people you admire.

4. In the library you will find the *World Almanac* or the *Statistical Abstract of the United States*. Look up the latest figures on the number of traffic deaths for a year in your state. Then look up the amount of money spent in your state for public school education. Do you see how such figures could be used in a speech?
5. Bring to class some unusual object that you have at home. Explain to us either its origin or its use.
6. Listen to a speech by an experienced speaker. Is it clear? Is it interesting? Is it appropriate?
7. Become interested in a controversial subject like Our Foreign Policy or The Coming Election. Collect and arrange all the arguments you can find pro and con. Note how well each argument supports the point it is selected to develop.

PREPARE YOUR INTRODUCTION AND CONCLUSION

HOW TO START AND HOW TO STOP

Now

the main part of your speech is ready. This is called the BODY. It is made up of your main points (with sub-points), which, in turn, are developed by your material.

But

how do you begin and end your speech?

Every speech has a beginning, the introduction, and an ending, the conclusion.

Whatever you say in the introduction should make us want to hear more.

Whatever you say in the conclusion should make us glad we did.

The Introduction

There are usually three things to do at the beginning of your talk.

First

Get the attention of your listeners by

—asking a question

What is a beatnik? Is he a sniveling, whining defeatist, or is he a prophet crying for redress from a goose-stepping, ignominious, materialistic society?

—telling a story

Whenever anyone asks me what a hypochondriac is, I tell him the story of a man who rushed into the doctor's office with a handkerchief over his ear. "Doctor, doctor," he howled, "I bit my ear!" "Don't be absurd," said the doctor. "How can a man bite his own ear?" "Why," replied the patient indignantly, "I stood on a chair"

—making a startling statement

We are not alone in the universe. At this moment signals from other civilizations are bombarding our earth. So convinced of this are our scientists that a world conference was held recently to discuss possible techniques for intercepting these signals from other worlds.

—referring to yourself

I was born in San Francisco. Among my earliest memories is the clang of the cable car as it busily hauled its passengers up and down the steep hills of the city. Fascinated and enchanted from childhood by its sights and sounds and smells, I would like to take you on a quick tour of this magical city.

—referring to your subject

At dawn of a summer morn, breakers at scores of beaches along hundreds of miles of California coast are plastered with flying boards carrying devotees of a new cult, *surfing*. All around America's wave-lapped perimeter—and even inland too—the scene is the same as more and more *surfers* become absorbed in the nation's fastest growing sport, a special kind of madness called *surfing*.

—saying something funny

A schoolboy once defined the spinal column as a pole; you sit on one end and your head sits on the other.

Next

Give us a reason for listening to you. Getting our attention is not enough. You want to hold our attention. If you give us a reason to believe that there are interesting things ahead, we will be looking forward expectantly to what is coming.

—(continuing the beatnik illustration)

Unless we are able to place the beatnik in his proper niche in history we can never be sure whether he is an object of ridicule or a harbinger of the wave of the future.

—(continuing the hypochondriac illustration)

We may laugh at the hypochondriac, but to him his ailments are real. Hypochondria is a form of mental illness so common that each of you may well have a friend or relative afflicted with it.

Then

Tell us where you are going and how you are going to get there. Give us a bird's-eye view of your speech.

—(continuing the beatnik illustration)

Today I wish to tell you about the writings of two leaders of the beat generation. When I finish, I am sure you will be able to put the beatnik in his proper place in history.

—(continuing the hypochondriac illustration)

It is my intention to talk to you about hypochondria, the imaginary ailment, describing some typical cases, telling you the several forms hypochondria may take and how it may be cured.

The Conclusion

Next to getting started on a speech the hardest thing to do is to stop.

Make the ending interesting, brief, and to the point.

Don't say the obvious.

That's the way I see it, anyway.
Well, thank you for listening.

Don't be trite.

Now I hope I've made my points clear.
In conclusion I would like to say. . . .

Instead

—sum up what you have said

I hope that I have succeeded in making these San Francisco scenes live in your imagination for these few minutes: the row of sidewalk kitchens on Fisherman's Wharf; the ghosts of the gold-diggers, of both sexes, that still lurk in the shadows of the Barbary Coast; the window displays of Chinatown that would make Marco Polo feel at home; and the welding of two traditions into one at the Presidio, the past of Spain and of America. They are all found in the city by the Golden Gate.

—make a final appeal

We must believe with William Faulkner that "man will not merely endure; he will prevail. It is not enough to believe that when the last ding-dong of doom has clanged and faded from the last worthless rock, hanging tideless in the last red and dying evening, that there will be one more sound: that of man's funny inexhaustible voice, still talking. I will not accept that! Man will not merely endure; he will prevail . . . because he has a soul, a spirit, capable of compassion and sacrifice and endurance."

—give a final example

And if the space age has not already captured you, let me tell you of one more plan. Already on the design boards is the space station. It will be a launching pad hundreds of miles out from the earth where satellites aimed at faraway planets will be able to start their journey; it will be a spaceship building yard, where prefabricated sections of satellites sent up from earth will be put together, and it will be a hotel too where space travelers will stop off for food, rest, and recreation and help as they explore the universe.

—tell a final story

Let me end this talk on our Alliance for Progress with our Latin American neighbors by telling you a story:

A certain man, on the way to Jericho, fell among thieves . . .

—use a quotation

Freedom of speech for those who disagree strongly with us makes us uncomfortable, but we must defend the rights of all to speak. One of the authors of the Bill of Rights, Thomas Jefferson, gave this reassurance in his First Inaugural Address. "If there be any among us who wish to dissolve this Union, or to change its republican form, let them stand undisturbed as monuments of the safety with which error of opinion may be tolerated when reason is left free to combat it."

—or issue a challenge

as Mr. Kennedy did in his Inaugural Address, "And so, my fellow Americans, ask not what your country can do for you—Ask what you can do for your country. My fellow citizens of the world: Ask not what America will do for you, but what together we can do for the freedom of man.

"Finally, whether you are citizens of America or citizens of the world, ask of us here the same high standards of strength and sacrifice which we ask of you. With a good conscience our only sure reward, with history the final judge of our deeds, let us go forth to lead the land we love, asking His blessing and His help, but knowing that here on earth God's work must truly be our own."

WHAT TO DO

Read a speech from a newspaper or from the magazine *Vital Speeches of the Day*. What did you think of the effectiveness of the introduction and the conclusion? Report on your reactions to the class.

During the next round of speeches, notice particularly the introductions and the conclusions. Comment to the class both on the least and on the most effective.

Write several introductions and conclusions for your next speech. Read them to a willing listener. Then select the best ones to use. Listen carefully to class comments after your speech.

CONSTRUCT YOUR OUTLINE

What you need now is some method for tying everything together, something that will serve as your guide from the first step of your preparation until you are ready to give your speech.

An outline will do this.
It should include

    —a good *title* for your *subject*
    —a statement of your *purpose*
    —the *plan* you are going to use
    —the *main points* of your plan
    —the *sub-points* (if any)
    —the *material supporting* these points
    —your *introduction* written out in full
    —your *conclusion* written out in full.

Here is a sample form.

_____
(title)

Subject: _____

Purpose: _____

The introduction

(Write out in full your opening remarks in which you get our attention, give us a reason for listening, and present us with a bird's-eye view of your talk.
You actually might do all of this in one or two sentences.)

The body

The plan

1. The first main point of your plan
   a. a sub-point
      (1) material supporting this point
      (2) more material supporting this point
      (3) more material supporting this point, etc.
   b. another sub-point, etc.

2. The second main point of your plan
   a. a sub-point
      (1) material supporting this point
      (2) more material supporting this point, etc.
   b. another sub-point, etc.

3. The third main point of your plan, etc.

The conclusion

(Write out in full your final remarks by which you either sum up what you have said, make a final appeal, or use some other technique by which you tie everything together.)

Here are two outlines that were used by students.

TIME ON OUR HANDS

Subject: The unwise use of our free time

Purpose: To persuade people to organize their free time properly

The introduction

Today I'm going to tell you a story about a man who did something we're all going to do. He died. And after he died

72

he found a surprising situation. There were people everywhere to wait on him. Someone brought him food, someone took him driving, someone even put on his clothes. At first the change was pleasant; then it became tolerable and finally it was downright boring. After an irritating and monotonous morning the man exclaimed, "If this is what Heaven is like, I'll go to Hell." The response came quickly, "Sir, this *is* Hell."

I'm not suggesting that you might soon have a similar experience, but are we not facing a situation that could lead to the same unhappy ending? Today, let's think about our increasing leisure time and the use we must make of it.

The body

Cause-effect plan

1. Americans have too much idle time.
    a. Automatic appliances and gadgets have freed the housewife.
    b. Automation devices have given the laborer a shorter work week.
    c. TV watching and other passive activities fill the idle hours.
2. Idleness can lead to discontent and unhappiness.
    a. Examples from history show that it is difficult for man to change his work habits.
    b. Research by a German industrialist revealed that many people were happier working a six-day week.
    c. A government study estimated that the future will bring even more leisure time.

The conclusion

The American people must remember that free time is not a natural way for them. They must learn to control free time as well as working time. Poor use of leisure time will lead to a situation similar to the man in our story: Heaven turned into Hell.

CRASH HELMETS

Subject: A new safety driving device

Purpose: To inform the class about what crash helmets are like and how they work

The introduction

The chances are that one out of every three members of this class will someday be in an automobile accident. Whether you survive or not will depend on many things. A member of this class has spoken to you on the purpose of the safety belt. I want to talk to you about another safety device: the crash helmet.

The body

Theory-practice plan (structure-function)
1. How it is constructed
   a. It is similar to a football helmet.
   b. The outer shell is plastic or fiberglas.
   c. The inside is a leather cap that fits on the head like a stocking cap.
   d. It feels as though you are wearing a slightly deflated basketball held in place by a chin strap.
2. How it works
   a. A blow on the head with a steel pipe is sensed but is not fatal.
   b. A friend on a motorcycle bought a crash helmet which three weeks later saved his life.
   c. A personal experience with a crash helmet has proven that it is valuable to a driver.

The conclusion

Crash helmets are absolutely necessary on the race track. Now that an increasing number of automobiles are on the road with stepped-up horsepower, they are also necessary on the highway. In the future, along with the safety belt, crash helmets may become standard equipment. And since there are many women drivers, some designer will come up with the bright idea of having the crash helmets match the car's interior.

The next outline is based on a speech given by Goodwin J. Knight, former governor of California, at a Governor's Conference on Youth and Narcotics.

THE NARCOTICS RACKET

Subject: The sale of narcotics to students

Purpose: To persuade young people to join the crusade against the sale and use of narcotics

The introduction

Today student leaders from schools all over Northern California are in attendance here. Here, you will have an opportunity to join in this crusade against one of the greatest evils of our time, the narcotics racket—the scourge that is taking such a terrible toll in happiness and health among our people.

The body

Problem-solution plan
(what plans do the sub-points follow?)

1. The dope peddler on campus
   a. His target
      i. incidents involving curious and daring young people
      ii. figures on profit on dope sold to young people
   b. His wares
      i. damaging barbituates called "goof balls"
      ii. dangerous benzedrines called "beenies"
      iii. the narcotics which lead to the "point-of-no-return"

2. How to destroy him
   a. Avoiding unknown substances
   b. Choosing associates with care
      i. example of consequence from making poor choices
      ii. more examples
   c. Making experimentation in drugs unpopular
      i. directions to students themselves
      ii. directions to parents and teachers

The conclusion

Dope peddlers represent a greater and a deadlier evil than a man with a loaded gun pointed right at your heart. You must learn how to stiff-arm an opponent like a dope peddler who is trying to tackle you before you even get started on your end run through life.

Here is an outline based on a twenty-minute speech by Senator Paul Douglas of Illinois.

FIVE GREAT AMERICANS

Subject: The contributions of five Americans who put public service before personal advancement

Purpose: To inspire the audience to have faith in our public servants and to strive themselves to be better representatives of democratic ideals

The introduction

In these days of denunciation and counterdenunciation, I thought it might be well tonight to speak about five Americans who are in danger of being forgotten, but who by their work and lives have helped to make us all better men and women.

The body

Topical plan

1. The first is the Quaker John Woolman, an anti-slavery leader.
   a. His awareness of the evils of slavery
   b. His travels over the country speaking against slavery
   c. His success in getting all Quakers to free their slaves

2. The second man is John Peter Altgeld, an honest politician.
   a. His attempts to obtain justice for the poor
   b. The story of his refusal of an enormous bribe
   c. A poem in his honor by Vachel Lindsay

3. The third person is Jane Addams, the founder of Hull House in the slums of Chicago.
   a. Her civic enterprises
   b. Her literary successes
   c. An evaluation of her character

4. The fourth selection is Senator Robert M. LaFollette.
   a. His early reforms in the state of Wisconsin
   b. His establishment of a genuine merit system for state employees

c. His reforms in Congress

5. The fifth selection is Senator George W. Norris of Nebraska.
   a. His successful efforts to pass needed progressive legislation
   b. A colleague's statement of his honesty

The conclusion

These Americans were bitterly attacked and criticized in their day, but their lives have stood the test of time. One hopes that mankind can recognize such men and women while they are living and not merely after they have died. I shall, close, therefore, with the final words of Bernard Shaw in his play, *Saint Joan*: "O God that madest this beautiful earth, when will it be ready to receive Thy saints? How long, O Lord, how long?"

HERE ARE SOME HINTS

1. The number of main points you make depends on the plan you are using. But if you think you need more than five you will find that you can usually combine your points or subdivide them.
2. When you *divide* your points you have *sub-points*. When you *develop* your points you have *supporting materials*.
3. The amount of supporting material you use depends on the length of your talk.
4. The kind of supporting material you use (definitions, stories, examples, etc.) depends on your knowledge of the topic and the interests of your listeners.
5. Be consistent in the wording of your outline. Either phrases or sentences may be in order, but be consistent in their use

—for example, phrases for the main points and sentences for the supporting material, or vice versa. Whether phrases or sentences, let there be just one per point.

6. Prepare your outline while you prepare your speech—not after.

HOW TO CHOOSE A VOCATION

Subject: ~~The~~ *Ways to meet the* problems arising when choosing a vocation.

Purpose: To inform students of some of the ways to choose a vocation.

The Introduction:
"What are you going to be when you grow up?" "Are you going to be a teacher like your mom?" "Are you going to be an engineer like your dad?" You have probably been asked these questions many times and you will be asked them again.

There are more than 30,000 different occupations open to you. To choose the right one ~~you must study yourself.~~ *let your home, your school, and your knowledge of yourself help you make the choice*

The Body:
1. Let your home help.
   a. ~~See what your family would like you to be.~~ *Parents' suggestions*
   b. Statistics on how many students choose their parents' vocations.
   c. ~~Don't be pushed into a vocation as John was.~~ *John's experience of being pushed into a vocation*
2. Let your school help.
   a. ~~Find out about as many jobs as you can.~~ *Information on jobs*
   b. Intelligence tests and aptitude tests available. *from library*
   c. Comparison between your physical abilities and physical requirements of jobs you are interested in.
3. ~~Know yourself.~~ *Let your self-knowledge help.*
   a. ~~Study your philosophy of life.~~ What means the most to you in life: ~~money, leisure, family relationships?~~ *The relationship between your philosophy of life and the kind of work you choose.*

The Conclusion:
After careful study and combining what you have found out about yourself you should have broken down your choice to a certain group or type of job and in time you can choose the one that appeals to you most. You should be proud of your choice and sure it is worth working for.

Choose a more interesting and meaningful last sentence

79

When your outline is finished

> —work out your speech with the outline in front of you until you've got it
> —think your speech through out loud
> —discard your outline, and
> —give your speech meaningfully.
> "Have a full realization of the content of the words as you utter them"

and have

"a lively sense of communication."[1]

Keep a small card with just a few key words on it to refer to—in case you need it.

WHAT TO DO

Check the outline for your speech with the samples given in this chapter. Ask the class to jot down what they think are your purpose, main points, and supporting material while you talk. If your outline doesn't agree with the ideas your listeners picked out, you may need to improve your plan or your material development or to make your ideas come through better when you talk.

With the rest of the class make an outline of some excellent speech to be found in your library. Then let the instructor go over this outline to see if you have made a complete and a correct analysis.

[1] Winans, James A. Speech Making (N.Y.: Appleton-Century-Crofts, 1938), 25.

CHOOSE YOUR LANGUAGE
THE WORDS YOU USE

When you talk, you express your meaning in words. We understand what you mean only insofar as you use the right words, the right grammar, the right pronunciation.

Here are some word hints:

Don't make "uh" noises when you run out of words.
Say nothing at all until you have the words ready.
When you say "uh" we think you're confused.
When you say nothing we think you're thinking.

It isn't the long word that is to be avoided so much as the *wrong* word. But don't strain for the big word.

Use words that sound like what they mean:

sticky fingers	icy water
rumbling trucks	a smashing blow
mournful music	whimpering child
a curt reply	slimy salamander.

Repeat key phrases for emphasis.

Martin Luther King, Jr. said,

"I have a dream today. It is a dream deeply rooted in the American dream.
"I have a dream that one day on the red hills of Georgia ...
"I have a dream that one day the state of Alabama ...
"I have a dream that one day even the state of Mississippi ...
"I have a dream that one day every valley will be exalted."

Use colorful rather than colorless words.

Instead of saying

The treacherous head of Fascist Italy . . .
Winston Churchill said,
"That jackel, Mussolini . . . !"

Instead of the trite

You must work if you wish to succeed

say

If you want to keep from being a stuffy old bore for forty odd years, you've got to learn to be something now. To be young and active at sixteen is no achievement; to be a respected person at sixty is.

We like to see, feel, taste, and touch what you say as well as hear it.

Instead of saying

All races join in fighting for our country
President Kennedy said,
"There are no 'white' or 'colored' signs on the foxholes or graveyards of battle."

Instead of saying

Our community is assisting in the anti-poverty program

say

The time is now. In a little house near Main Street, converted for office use, there are three or four people at work, setting in motion a challenging socialized experiment, a War on Poverty.

Strive for balance and beauty in sentence composition.

Kennedy said,
"Geography has made us neighbors. History has made us friends. Economics has made us partners, and necessity has made us allies."

Contrive memorable epigrams.

> Earl Warren said,
> "There is a law beyond the law. It calls upon us to be fair in business, when the law cannot command fairness; it bids us temper justice with mercy, when the law can only enforce justice; it demands our compassion for the unfortunate, although the law can only give him his legal due. There is a law beyond the law as binding as the law itself."

Use clear-cut connectives between your main points:

> Not only . . . but also . . .
> Now let us consider still another argument.
> In the second place
> On the other hand
> In addition to this
> For example
> Now that we have . . . let us . . .

Don't make common mistakes in grammar, such as

> Between you and I
> He don't know it
> These kind of things
> Do like I do
> Winston tastes good like a cigarette should.
> He can't hardly
> If you were me
> Everyone is asked to do their part.

Don't make conspicuous mispronunciations, such as,

> athletic (athaletic)
> influence (accent on second syllable)
> experiment (expeariment)
> picture (pitcher)
> column (colyum).

Avoid careless and slovenly pronunciations such as,

sittin	lotta
jist	git
probly	kep.

Seldom use slang; rarely use "bromides"; never be vulgar.

Some words offend certain people nearly as much as profanity:

lousy	you guys
guts	belly
eats (noun)	stinks.

Use the language of conversation. Use the pronouns we, our, us. It will help us to realize that you are talking *with* us, not *at* us.

Say

This is our problem. We must do something about it or face the consequences.

Avoid emotion-loaded words. Unless you define them such words have many meanings:

Americanism, pink (meaning liberal), reactionary (meaning conservative), strait-laced, red blooded.

Let your language be accurate, forceful, honest, and it will be right.

WHAT TO DO

Why not

—keep a list of words that you are using incorrectly
—keep a list of words that you are adding to your vocabulary
—keep a list of words that sound like what they mean
—keep a list of words that make pictures in our minds.

Why not

> write out your next speech, and write it as you plan to say it? Write with your ear rather than your eye. How the speech "listens" is more important than how it "looks."

Then

> exchange written speeches with another member of the class. Read his speech carefully, checking his language for correctness, forcefulness, and naturalness. Rewrite your own speech to improve the language. Then give it.

CONTROL YOUR BODY
WHAT TO DO WITH IT

Remember that you don't just talk with your mouth. You talk with all of you.

Here are some body hints:

Walk to the front

    —don't run.
    —Don't creep either.

Wait until you are standing in front of us before you start talking, and wait until you have finished before you start walking to your seat.

Think of your whole body as one piece; then it won't fall to pieces.

Stand up straight

> —but not too stiffly
> —and not too sloppily.

Look at each one of us while you are talking

> —not out of the window
> —not out of the door
> —not out of focus.

Move around only when it makes sense

> —when you have finished
> with one point and are
> going on to the next, or
> —when you have finished
> talking before one sec-
> tion of your audience
> and are going on to the
> next.

Don't hide behind the furniture.

Don't hold the speaker's stand in a death grip.

Keep your feet fairly close together and your weight on both feet.

Don't take care of your hands; let your hands take care of themselves. They're fastened on and will stay down at your sides by themselves if you will let them.

They can't gesture if you handcuff them

    —by holding one hand with the other
    —by putting them behind your back
    —or by putting both hands in your pocket.

When they do gesture

    —to describe something or
    —to bring home a point,

let them follow through as far as they will go—all the way.

Don't make embryonic twitches as if your arms were strapped to your sides.

Don't make movements that have nothing to do with your talk.

Don't forget that you put over the idea with *all* of you!

The expression on your face tells us a lot about you, so

—look pleasant, not grim
—be sincere, not silly
—look enthusiastic, not bored

for

your face reveals the real you.

WHAT TO DO

1. To make you feel comfortable in front of us, you might try
   —using your hands and body to show us how to do something like hitting a golf ball, bowling, dancing, hairstyling, boxing

   or

   —using your hands and body to make a story come alive. Show us how tall or short people are. Show how someone moves. Act out what happens.

2. Practice moving around in your next speech—as you go from one main point in your speech plan to the next; maybe, from one detail to the next.

3. Show us all the ways to stand, walk, look, and move that distract from speech ideas. Watch for such distractions as you see and listen to speakers. Keep your own list of movements that distract us while you are talking.

4. Try reading a clever story in front of us while someone erases the chalk board or walks around behind you. Do you see how important movement is (even though it is the wrong kind)?

IMPROVE YOUR VOICE
HOW TO USE IT

Remember that we depend on your voice to get your ideas.
We must be able to *hear* you and to *understand* you.

Here are some voice hints:

Make your vowel tones strong and clear, especially

the *ahs* as in "father"
the *aws* as in "fought"
the *ohs* as in "foam"
the *oohs* as in "food"
the *eehs* as in "feed"
the *ays* as in "*fade.*"

Let your nasal tones hum and ring:
the *m-m-ms*, the *n-n-ns* and the
*ng*s.

Form your consonants accurately
and distinctly.

91

Use plenty of lip action in such words as,

whisk broom
memorable
vulnerable.

Use adequate jaw action in such words as,

orangutan
yellow
powerful.

Use adequate tongue action in such words as,

secretary
particularly
volume
peculiarly
behavioral.

Open your mouth.

You are much much more conspicuous when you *don't* open your mouth than when you do. Practice in front of a mirror and see for yourself.

Yell

yeow, yeow, yeow, yeow
walla, walla, walla, walla
crotchety, crotchety, crotchety

and open your mouth!

WARNING

Never strain your voice when practicing this way. Yell easily.

Remember

that if you make a monkey of yourself in practice, you are more likely to be a human being in public.

Control your breathing.

See how long you can count on one breath.
Can you go to fifteen? Twenty?
Don't cheat!
Count loudly and slowly!
It's not the *amount* of air you use but the way you control it that's important.

Relax your throat.

Get a yawning feeling inside
your throat.
Get a vibrating tone inside
your head.
"Chuck" yourself under the
chin while speaking. It
should always be "squashy"
and flexible under there.

Project your voice.

See how far away you can be heard with the least possible effort.
See how loud you can count without straining.
If you've learned to control your breathing, and to get your tone to vibrate, you can talk as loud as you want.

Bring out the meaning of your idea.

Stress the important words.
Pause before the important words.
Keep within the speed limit.
(Don't talk too fast; don't talk too slowly.)
Change your speed.
(It's as monotonous to speak too slowly as it is to speak too fast all the time.)

Change your pitch.
 (Go up and down as you do in conversation.)

The meaning will be lost if you try to impress us with your tones

                    or

imitate the tones of a "model" orator.

Talk *with* us, not *at* us or *to* us.

WHAT TO DO

1. Try reading a news item in different ways. Read it slowly. Sounds serious, doesn't it? Read it rapidly. Gayer, isn't it? Combine the two for interest.

2. See what happens when you emphasize different words in a sentence. Try this sentence: "I'm glad you're here this evening."

3. Carry on a conversation using the letters of the alphabet in place of words. Now, tell your favorite story using the letters of the alphabet instead of words. Notice how the change in pitch carries the idea.

4. Read a short selection on the tape recorder. How does your voice rate for each of the following?

    clarity
    quality
    projection
    emphasis
    variety
How can you improve it?

5. Listen to the recording of voices in Volume 11 of *I Can Hear It Now*, edited by Edward R. Murrow. How do you rate these voices?

6. Become voice-conscious. Listen to your friends' voices, your instructors' voices, and voices of your favorite entertainers. Comment on them in class.

BUILD YOUR SELF-CONFIDENCE
HOW TO KEEP FROM BEING SCARED

Self-confidence will develop as you develop right attitudes. A speech is not a solo performance nor an act, but a sharing of ideas with others. You must have something *worth while to say* that *should be said* and *said by you*. Feel impelled to speak out!

Here are some nerve hints:

It is normal to feel tense before you speak. That is nature's way of warming up. A good speaker, like a good race horse, must be keyed up to do the job well.

Think of us instead of yourself while talking. Be sure we're "getting it." If you are conscious of others you are not self-conscious. And if you are not self-conscious you are not scared.

Self-confidence will develop with preparation, so be prepared.

—Know *what* you are going to say.
—Know *why* you are going to say it.
—Know your *plan*.
—Select supporting material to develop each point well in advance.
—Know how to *start* and how to *stop*.
—Use an *outline* to guide your preparation from the beginning to the end. You won't need it when you give your speech.
—Think through your talk, and practice aloud until you *know* you've got it.
—Put everything you have into everything you say.
—*Speak out* clearly, distinctly, forcefully.

WHAT TO DO

Give an impromptu talk on a subject given you just before you speak. Can you?

Take part in a class discussion on Fear, Stage Fright, and Tension.

Join a discussion group—or form one. Learn to think aloud whenever you are with others.

Speak whenever you can, in club, student government, church, or committee meetings. Be sure what you say fits in, whether it is one sentence or ten.

EVALUATE YOUR PROGRESS
WATCH YOUR IMPROVEMENT

Be content to improve in some way with each speech. Take notice of any sudden improvement in the class and in yourself. Use the comments of your teachers and classmates to guide you in your aims.

Keep a record of your improvement
each time.

	Outstanding	Effective	Average	Weak	Inadequate
Subject					
Purpose					
Plan					
Material					
Introduction					
Conclusion					
Language					
Body					
Voice					
Self-confidence					

Check your speech *before* giving it.

		Check One		
		Yes	No	Uncertain
Your subject	Is it suited to us?			
	Is it suited to you?			
	Is it suited to the time allowed?			
Your purpose—	Do you accomplish it?			
Your plan—	Does it suit your purpose?			
	Is it easy to follow?			
	Does it reveal the main points of your speech?			
Your material—	Is it clear?			
	Is it interesting?			
	Is it appropriate?			
Your introduction—	Does it get our attention?			
	Does it arouse our interest?			
	Does it give us a bird's-eye view?			
Your conclusion—	Is it succinct?			
	Is it final enough?			
	Is it interesting?			

		Check One		
		Yes	No	Uncertain
Your language—	Have you chosen the best words and phrases?			
	Is your speech grammatical?			
	Is your pronunciation acceptable?			
	Are your transitions apt?			
	Is your language imaginative?			
Your body—	Does it match your ideas?			
	Is it coordinated?			
	Is your movement meaningful?			
Your voice—	Is it audible?			
	Is it understandable?			
	Is it pleasant?			
Your self-confidence—	Have you the right attitudes?			
	Do you feel adequately prepared?			